MW00472863

LIVING WITH AN
ALCOHOLIC

LIVING WITH AN ALCOHOLIC

MY STORY OF HEALING
AND THE
BAHÁ'Í FAITH

Joyce B. Lakewood

© 2017
Copyright is held by Special Ideas
on behalf of the author who has
written under a pseudonym
in order to protect her privacy
and that of her family.

Published by Special Ideas
Heltonville IN
www.special-ideas.com
1-800-326-1197

ISBN 978-1-888547-38-2

Table of Contents

This book is addressed to confused and suffering Bahá'ís, their fellow community members, and Bahá'í Institutions who want to better understand some of the experiences of people dealing with addictions such as alcoholism, and the related problems, as well as the recovery methods and choices they might choose to use and take. People investigating the Bahá'í Faith who are also involved with addiction and recovery issues may also find it helpful to use.

OVERVIEW

There is a strange duality that sometimes occurs in the Bahá'í Faith. There is one side where we want everyone who encounters the Bahá'í Faith to already be perfectly a Bahá'í. The other is where we want everyone, once they are a Bahá'í, to be able to very quickly live up to the high standards of the Teachings (We think this would save everyone so much trouble!). All the while we have this inner knowledge, that we often try to deny, that we cannot possibly live up to all the Teachings ourselves. Sound familiar to anyone?

Well, welcome to a dose of reality...the world is a place where many seekers and Bahá'ís are suffering from the effects of a variety of illnesses, and denial after a while tends to cause a mess. There are alcoholics, drug addicts, the physically or sexually abused and abusers, the mentally ill, the anorexic or bulimic, and every other challenge. There are also multiple family members and friends negatively affected by these diseases and conditions. They all need the healing power of Bahá'u'lláh's message (the Prophet-Founder of the Bahá'í Faith), help from professionals and support groups, and the support of a loving community and its Institutions. It's not easy, but necessary, as best as we can.

The Bahá'í Faith is all about unity, and what often keeps people distant from each other or disunified is lack of understanding. Even if people cannot totally identify with the experiences and choices of others, the possibility exists to be lovingly supportive and accepting, thereby bridging the distance.

When we don't understand, judgment and disapproval can become the norm, and hearts are bruised and souls estranged. Often people struggling with the emotional impact of these illnesses and problems are very fragile, and they need words and actions chosen with care. It is also important for everyone who is relating with or doing counseling with the individuals involved to understand that recovery is a one-day-at-a-time process, with successes and failures, progress and relapses, perseverance, pain, and joy. Like any process of personal transformation, the struggle takes a lifetime of effort. In our world that increasingly expects instant everything, sometimes it's hard to remember that building trust, making changes, and focusing on healing all takes time.

A common problem that interferes with help and healing for the suffering individual, the family members, and the community is denial. Any or all of these people or groups can consciously or unconsciously avoid admitting that there is a problem. Facing a problem and taking actions to address it, are often difficult and painful. It often seems easier to run away. Knocking down denial causes change. Sometimes significant emotional pain can occur when this protective mechanism is removed, and it may seem for a while that things have become worse rather than better.

Relationships do not stay the same after denial lessens, and people often have to make major adjustments in their lives that require hard work, strong emotions, and commitments of time and finances. There are often significant fears about failure, losing friendships and relationships, doing the "wrong thing," and so on. The key point to remember is that the health and circumstances of all those affected have far less possibility of changing for the better, and in fact will likely get worse, as long as the parties involved are in denial and dancing around the obvious. Running away becomes a less viable option when we realize that we would take many of our problems with us.

Bahá'ís are to be seekers of truth and light, so institutions and individuals are wise to take the responsibility for reading about and understanding the problems that are brought to them, as well as turning to experts for help. Addictions, in particular, are such a mixture of mental, physical, emotional, and spiritual aspects, that knowledge in addressing the issues surrounding them is very important. This book does not attempt to educate on specific illnesses. Books abound by experts in the various fields, and I urge you to turn to them for understanding. It's also important to remember as you read this that even where something is written from the perspective of dealing with a specific disease, such as alcoholism, there are often strong similarities for both the suffering person and those around him/her when faced with other illnesses and problems, such as eating disorders, physical or sexual abuse, drug addiction, and so on.

I have experienced profound emotional pain in my life along with numerous tests, but I have found learning opportunities each time...sometimes slower than other times...but learning is always a possibility! A curious phenomenon has also been a regular occurrence: Each time I learn something, God then puts someone in my path who needs to know what I have learned in order to work through his/her own pain. Part of the purpose of this book is the realization that I need to share some of this learning.

So, I ask for your openness and for you to reserve judgment...simply listen with your heart and mind to the experience, strength, hope, and learning that follow to see if they are helpful. This will not represent all perspectives or everyone's experience with recovery, because each is unique. Hopefully my story will share enough universal experience that you can identify with or understand at least parts of it. By the Grace of God, this understanding might then translate into positive action in the wonderful, growing, and tested community of Bahá'u'lláh.

MY STORY

I knew nothing about alcoholism or mental illness before meeting Jerry, my to-be husband, at age 19 when he was 25. There were warning signs during our courtship, but I didn't realize what was going on. Once he tricked me into taking a drink. He would call me when he had been drinking and challenge me on whether I loved him. He threatened suicide if I broke up with him. I just kept praying that marriage would make it all better.

When we met with my parents to discuss their giving consent to our marrying (a requirement for Bahá'ís), my father asked whether alcohol might be a concern. Baha'is are not permitted to drink alcohol, but Jerry was not a Bahá'í. I answered the question instead of letting him do it, saying that no, there was no problem, only occasional social drinking. That was all I saw, as he was hiding his heavy drinking; and I was unwilling to face any doubts about our marrying in any case. I didn't see Jerry drink heavily until our honeymoon. Only years later did I realize he had been heavily drinking since age 14.

Denial of the issues was a theme from the beginning. When my husband was actively drinking, I often felt that if I said the wrong thing I would make things worse, so I did not say anything. What I learned in the process of getting help was that in my case, my denial and withdrawal made my husband more angry and violent and made it much more difficult for either of us to get help. Counseling and a support group was necessary to help me express appropriate things at appropriate times.

A note of caution is important here, because every situation has differences. Any time violence is a possibility, care in communication is critical, and outside help is probably essential. Some family members in serious situations can become very angry and vocal, increasing the risk for violence. It's often important to wait and try communications only when the alcohol level has subsided, and there is a greater chance of communicating successfully.

I did not understand enough about alcoholism to recognize that most of the difficulties we were experiencing in our marriage were connected to the drinking. I thought that it was just a part of the problem. We tried many solutions, such as buying a house, having a baby, and making job changes. Geographical cures—moving to try to make things better—were a way of life.

My functioning consisted of burying myself in romance novels or letters from old boyfriends—trying to find some escape from reality, hiding under the covers of the bed, and barely handling mothering responsibilities. My husband's threats of suicide and violence kept me scared and upset. Although I knew on some level that the drinking was a problem, I often denied to myself just how serious it was. I had stopped trusting God and stopped praying. I had little connection to the Bahá'í community, and certainly no one I felt I could turn to for help. I thought that telling my family members, who were all Bahá'ís, what was going on was not an option. I was not in an area served by a Local Spiritual Assembly (an elected council), and I had abandoned all my friends as things got worse in our home.

In many ways, I became a "non-person". I put on a different face and personality depending on the circumstances I was in, the wishes of those I was with, and what I thought I should be like. Behind these varying masks, I was terrified that if the masks were removed, there would be virtually no one left.

I began to see that I needed help.

One of my primary motivations for getting help was wanting to break the recurring generational cycle in our extended family. My husband was at least the third generation to have problems with alcohol. As I looked at my then 2-year-old daughter, I felt great fear for her future. There was a far greater chance for her if I got help; she was better off having at least one functioning parent.

A neighbor mentioned in a conversation that her husband had gone to a 12-Step family support group called Al-Anon Family Groups when his ex-wife was drinking. I was astonished that there might actually be help for my mess. I grabbed Al-Anon like a lifeline for a while, then left it and went back to hell for a few months.

During my time away from Al-Anon, things deteriorated terribly. Jerry's behavior included:

- · verbal assaults on my ability to think
  or make decisions
- · out-of-control spending
- · forcing me with violent sex
- · lack of fathering time
- · angry threats against neighbors
- · isolating me from friends and family
- · insistence on perfection in all areas
- · inability to hear any opinion but his own
- · threats to divorce me and take our daughter
  away from me

All these things took a huge physical, mental, emotional, and spiritual toll on me. I was desperate to find a way out, but unable to function well enough to take action. I involved my mother-in-law in the mess to an extent, but I really felt very alone. I did not believe that I had anyone to leave our daughter with while I went to get help, I did not feel I could spend family money to get counseling, and I could not think clearly enough to know what to do or where to go. I finally decided to write the National Spiritual Assembly of the Bahá'ís of the United State and ask for assistance, however, because divorce was starting to look like a possibility. They connected me to the closest Local Spiritual Assembly, which was about an hour away from me.

This Local Spiritual Assembly reached out to me by sending two of their members to meet with me. They also indicated if I chose to leave they could provide a safe house with a Bahá'í family for my daughter and me. Their support gave me some hope. I did choose to leave and stay with this family for a while. All nine members of the Assembly met with me and we prayed together. They were quite uncertain, however, about how to help me. An incident made it clear that Jerry was a potential danger to the family I was staying with, so my daughter and I moved to a hotel for a few days. After my husband agreed to go to Alcoholics Anonymous (AA) meetings, I agreed to return home.

I resented the Assembly for a long time because they did not "fix" everything for me. It was many years later that I realized that within days of their meeting and praying with me, I was back in Al-Anon, my husband attempted sobriety for the first time, and we were getting marriage counseling. I finally figured out that the Assembly was divinely guided...just differently than I expected! This time I vowed to never let go of the Al-Anon program because I was not willing to live in hell ever again. Al-Anon meetings were a safe place for me to talk, cry, and begin to understand the insanity of our lives. It was here that I got the message that I had to do what I could to get better, *regardless* of Jerry's choices or what happened to him.

At that point, we moved to an area a few hours away. I found a new Al-Anon group there. My husband stayed in AA for a while, but then went back to drinking. The city had a Local Spiritual Assembly, and I was elected to serve on it. I absolutely did not want anyone to know about home problems, though. Jerry was still extremely resentful about the Assembly I had consulted with earlier.

There is something about dysfunction, though, that just starts to leak out after a while. I kept doing things like bursting into tears after Assembly meetings, or getting too deeply into personal problems brought to the Assembly, or not having anyone over to our home. My functioning as an Assembly member was often destructive. If I thought a male Assembly member sounded like, acted like, or looked at me like my alcoholic husband, I reacted to him as if they were the same person. At the time, a number of people on the Assembly had grown up with alcoholism or been affected by it. What a mess some of our consultations became! Eventually we figured out that we were all troubled people at various stages of getting or not getting help.

At home, Jerry's drinking worsened. He was drinking on the job and in his car. He became so hostile to the Faith that he started insisting I not attend Bahá'í meetings and our daughter not attend Bahá'í children's classes. He also began threatening to throw away or burn my Bahá'í books. I was grateful to have an Assembly willing to give me clear guidance. They helped me set priorities and moderate my Bahá'í activities so that I was able to be part of community activities and service, without overdoing it and making problems at home worse. This moderation included things like attending Feasts but not going to Holy Day celebrations.

A notation I made at the time illustrates my state of mind: "Everything feels like it's splitting at the seams. I have this big pile of responsibilities and things I'm supposed to do but all I feel like doing is crying and kicking and hitting and shouting and pounding on something....I feel like things are at war in me and it scares the hell out of me. I'm afraid—I don't want it all to come flying out at my family...I just want it all to go away."

The Bahá'í teachings about divorce terrified me. When I was already in a defeated and hopeless place, it was very difficult to hear [my interpretation] that if I initiated leaving him and seeking divorce I would "unquestionably fall into great difficulties [and] become the victim of formidable calamities and experience deep remorse" ('Abdu'l-Baha, *Lights of Guidance*, #1306). I thought if I left Jerry, then I was obviously the cause of the divorce, of course. There were also many quotations about what type of marriage I was supposed to be building, so I just kept trying. One of the sad things about being in the state I was in, was that the Bahá'í Writings came through that filter. This meant I often heard and understood the Teachings in an unbalanced way, and I did not really know how to apply them to my life.

Most people suffering from or associated with addictions seem to have problems with low self-respect. Often this is as a direct result of mental, emotional, physical, or sexual abuse. I was no exception. I lacked confidence in my ability to function as a woman, mother, family member, community member, student, or employee. If someone asked me how I was, I would answer with information about my husband. I wasn't living my own life; I was submerged in someone else's life. Sometimes it was impossible to read and accept some of the Writings without taking them personally instead of putting them in their historical and proper perspective. In particular, some of the selections from the *Hidden Words* caused me difficulties. When I would read phrases like, "children of dust," "children of negligence", "O weed that springeth out of dust", or "O heedless ones", I would immediately feel worse about myself.

It does not take much study on anyone's part to discover that the Bahá'í Faith has very high standards. In addition, the life of 'Abdu'l-Bahá, who His grandson Shoghi Effendi states is our "Perfect Exemplar" is tough to live up to consistently. For many years of my life I felt that unless I (and everyone else too!) could do it all perfectly, I was always woefully inadequate, never good enough. Much of this I learned from the standards of my parents and grandparents. This need for perfectionism set me up to try to behave according to a standard of perfection on the surface, but with a non-existent sense of self-respect on the inside.

My drive for perfection also caused me to be highly judgmental of any actions of others or myself that did not measure up to my pre-determined standards. Can you imagine how loving and unified a community meeting was when I got angry at people for showing up late?! God fixed that one so I learned a lesson. I had to start showing up late because everyone in the community had car trouble for a while, and I had to use my car and pick people up so they could be there. I finally saw that being together was more important than being on time if I had to choose.

When things at home became increasingly out of control, I unconsciously began trying to exert control and impose order everywhere else in my life. At times this manifested itself as being rigidly insistent that my fellow employees adhere to the exact times set for lunch, trying to control the outcome of consultations in Assembly meetings, finding a lot of activities to direct and influence outside of our home, and over-caretaking situations that were not my business.

When I tried to control other people because Jerry's behavior was uncontrollable, the result was resentment, disunity, and conflict. Changing this pattern required careful self-awareness, listening to feedback from friends, asking myself if I was looking after my responsibilities or someone else's, and reminding myself that God was in charge, not me.

Jerry finally achieved sobriety after therapy, multiple stays in hospitals and treatment centers, and being in and out of AA. We had been married eight years at that point, and our daughter was age six. However, as time went by, it became increasingly apparent that the alcoholism had been hiding other, including multiple mental illnesses, severe depression, and multiple eating disorders. Jerry constantly threatened suicide and attempted it at least twice. He surprised us by becoming a member of the Bahá'í Faith after a suicide attempt. It helped his functioning and our marriage to an extent, but most of the problems remained.

I became the financial support for the family and went back to school part-time to obtain a degree. Throughout I struggled with whether to leave the marriage, but I always felt guilty about "abandoning" Jerry because he was sick. Every time things got terrible, he would make an attempt to get better. However, I was constantly afraid that he would take our daughter and run, and I would lose her and be unable to protect her. Jerry and I separated at times, but we kept coming back together and trying again.

Attempting to live in these circumstances while maintaining my own sanity became increasingly difficult. As our daughter approached age 18, I began to experience what I later discovered were symptoms of post-traumatic stress disorder (PTSD). I was having nightmares, anxiety attacks, and difficulty functioning at work. I finally moved out. Our very difficult divorce went through over the 18 months that followed. He tried marriage more times; he has since passed away.

FINDING SOME SOLUTIONS

When I first went to Al-Anon Family Groups, I asked them to help me prevent Jerry from becoming an alcoholic. I was years too late! The message back to me, however, was that I was not to worry about labeling him alcoholic or not; he would decide at some point if the label fit him. If his drinking was causing me a problem, then I needed help, regardless of his choices. What was important for me to hear was that I had not caused him to drink, I couldn't cure him, and I could not control his drinking. I could start working on my obsession with his drinking and getting help for me. If I removed denial from our home, this could prompt him to get help as well.

It is my certain belief that finding the Al-Anon 12-Step program literally saved my life—physically, mentally, emotionally, and spiritually. The disease of alcoholism in our home had caused me to stop functioning in healthy ways, reject a God Who I believed was punishing me unfairly, and set up a distance between myself and Bahá'u'lláh. Until I received help with and guidance about the illness, I could not pray or find the means of connecting with the Bahá'í community...the gap was too wide, and I could not see any way across to the other side.

Within my first few support meetings, I began to make changes. I stopped reading romance novels all day for escape, started paying more attention to my child, got out of the middle of the relationship between our child and her father, and listened when my Al-Anon group told me I could not survive living with alcoholism without God. Since God for me was the Bahá'í Faith, I spiritually re-entered the community. I had not officially resigned—after all what would everyone think?! My parents were well known...this would be terrible! I started to really read the Bahá'í Writings at this point too. I had been in a Bahá'í home for most of my growing-up years, but I had absorbed the Bahá'í atmosphere more often than studied its Teachings. So, I started to get spiritually on track.

In addition to the needed help I received in recovering and staying connected to the Faith, a marvelous synergistic side benefit occurred. My involvement with a 12-Step Program and the Bahá'í Faith both together in many ways helped me to be a better Bahá'í. In particular I increased my understanding of relying on God's Will and developed the tools to increase my self-knowledge and self-responsibility. Both groups are strong advocates of prayer and conscious contact with God (most 12-Step groups refer to Him as a Higher Power) and have strong commitments to unity as being vital for the health of the whole.

I was able to consistently attend Al-Anon meetings and asked two women to be my sponsors—trusted group members who share experience, strength, and hope and who help others understand the recovery program and how to recover. These women were vital in my recovery, and they also reached out lovingly to my daughter. I also sought therapy with a psychologist. This helped me to be less emotionally withdrawn and start confronting some of the destruction in our home. Withdrawing from conflict was a pattern I had learned from my earliest years at home...a good lesson for me in not blaming everything on the alcoholic!

Each step forward brought me closer to freedom. It is difficult to adequately convey the importance of this, but I will try. Finding out that I did not cause the problem and that alcoholism was a disease, was the first weight off my shoulders. Then I began the process of becoming truly me rather than pretending I was someone others wanted me to be. The steps of Al-Anon that helped me do a personal inventory of myself; share the good and bad with God, and with someone else to get perspective; and begin to change and make amends to those I had hurt. All of this began to free me from guilt, shame, and blame.

I became hopeful that I could grow up and be a mature adult. I learned in Al-Anon that I had to take care of myself and not neglect my health. I went to the dentist for the first time in years, started eating and sleeping properly, and protected my safety and rights as much as possible. I was able to start setting limits, such as refusing to allow him to take away my house key, purse, or block my car in the driveway. I became good at making alternate plans...and making spare sets of keys! I started learning about developing virtues in a sane and balanced way, not with my old perfectionistic style. I could actually be a functioning, serving member of the world and my Bahá'í community. Community members applauded the first time I was late for something—instead of rigidly, compulsively early—hugged me when I was in pain, and reached out to my husband when he would let them.

A significant amount of healing happened for me when someone shared a book with me written by David Seamands, a Christian minister, that was called "Healing for Damaged Emotions." He wrote a chapter in it that described perfectionism as a "spiritual distortion" involving extremes of guilt and conscience; the tyranny of the "oughts" and "shoulds"; the low self-respect from constant self-depreciation; the anxiety; the rigid legalism and inflexible insistence on rules and regulations; and the anger against self, others, and an impossibly demanding God. The author described individuals cursed with perfectionism as being at high risk for a breakaway or a breakdown because of the high stress of "trying to live with a self he can't like, a God he can't love, and other people he can't get along with." His cure? God's Grace...His loving acceptance of us that has nothing to do with worthiness. God never stops loving us.

Self-respect and self-confidence started to be possible for me as I followed the guidance of everyone trying to help me. I resumed studying for the degree I had never finished and was promoted at work. Each time I learned to do something new or had a success at college or work, I fought a little way back up from my state of miserable worthlessness. Some quotations from the Writings have helped reinforce the importance of continuing to make an effort to improve this area of my life. Bahá'u'lláh affirms God's positive view of us. He promotes human beings as "the noblest and most perfect of all created things" who have received the "radiance of all His names and attributes" and should be considered as a "mine rich in gems of inestimable value." (*Gleanings from the Writings of Bahá'u'lláh*, pp. 179, 65, and 260)

'Abdu'l-Bahá also says that "man's supreme honor and real happiness lie in self-respect, in high resolves and noble purposes, in integrity and moral quality, in immaculacy of mind." (*The Secret of Divine Civilization*, p. 19) These positive words have helped to restore my own self-respect and support others as they re-build their own self-worth. Because God encompasses the full range of qualities such as Mercy, Justice, Love, Joy, and Kindness, and I am created in His image, I have worked and can continue to work towards developing these qualities. Starting to see myself as "noble" instead of "worthless trash" was a wonderful gift.

The 12 Steps

Alcoholics Anonymous (AA) was the first to develop a set of 12 steps designed to help alcoholics stay sober and change their lives. Many other groups have since adopted the 12 Steps of AA, and with slight modifications, applied them to a multitude of other diseases and problems. (See the Appendices)

Steps 1 to 3 are designed to help members understand that their own human resources are not enough to solve their problems. God, or a Higher Power, is needed to work with them. Step 4 starts the path of taking significant action towards changing themselves by taking an inventory of their lives and their positive qualities and areas for growth. This step is reinforced by Steps 5, 6 and 7 which guide them through the process of overcoming personal faults that have caused many of their problems. Steps 8 and 9 again require action so that members are no longer burdened by guilt, a lack of forgiveness, and confusion. Step 10 addresses the ongoing maintenance of their characters as started in Step 4. Step 11 affirms the importance of prayer and meditation in staying in connection with God. Step 12 invites them to awaken themselves spiritually, practice these positive principles in their lives, and share healing with others.

When I joined Al-Anon, the 12 Steps initially represented something that I had to go through in their exact order and "pass," never to come back to again. I learned, however, that as each new challenge arose in my life and the lives of those close to me, and as each new problem surfaced in my husband, I needed to go back to the beginning and apply them all over again. I learned to grab whichever Step applied to whatever was troubling me at any particular time and apply it. The important thing for me was to make sure I became well enough to apply all of them at some point or another.

Step 1

We admitted we were powerless over alcohol—that our lives had become unmanageable.

The devastation of fruitlessly trying over and over again to control what seemed so awful and kept affecting me with so much pain brought me back again and again to the point of surrender. No matter what I wanted to be different, my powers to change them were often very limited. If I did not stop to recognize that my trying to change the unchangeable had made life unmanageable for myself again, I would have ended up with a broken head from banging it against a brick wall. I was dealing with people who were children of God, who were making choices that they alone were responsible for before God. Only He could hold them accountable in the end, and my controlling attitude and actions only made them resentful and unhappy at my interference.

I still had to set boundaries of safety and sanity around myself. I also had to clearly say at times that some behavior or another was unacceptable. However, the outcome was between them and God, and my motive could not be trying to force a solution.

I was filled with such sorrow and pain when I saw my loved one making choices that were bringing him awful consequences or which would bring him pain and possibly death. I thought, "How can I not do something to make a difference?" Then I thought about the things that really make a difference, that were bringing manageability back into my life and the situation: prayer, sharing love with him (which I sometimes had to pray to feel!), turning to an Assembly, my Al-Anon sponsors, or others for assistance, letting him live his life, and letting go so I could live mine. His life was not what I would choose for him or myself, but God gave us free will to make our own choices, not so that others could make them for us. We each on our own had to come to the realization that our lives lived without God and a recovery program were filled with insanity, and only with His healing was there hope. Pain and healing are a matched pair.

Step 2

Came to believe that a Power greater than ourselves could restore us to sanity.

Anxiety, fear, and confusion had me behaving in ways that made no sense. I felt as if I were walking around at all times with a cloud of gray anxiety over my head, always afraid of terrible things happening. Every siren was probably because Jerry was in an accident. Every phone call was surely bad news. I was so confused that I would do things such as calling the bank and finding out they were closed, and then going to the bank, forgetting they were closed. I allowed my child in the car with an active alcoholic. I cut myself off from family and friends. I sat and listened as I was verbally battered, and I accepted what was said as truth. I suffered through threats and acts of violence.

When I turned to the Bahá'í Writings for help, all I could understand was that I was responsible for trying to build a wonderful Bahá'í marriage and would be held responsible for all eternity if I initiated a divorce. I felt it was wrong to separate myself from someone who was sick. I was afraid what would happen to our daughter if there was a custody battle. Jerry kept telling me that I would lose her through the courts or him taking her and disappearing.

There was no question that I was a mess. I had no choice, I had to turn to a "Power greater than myself" to guide me back to sanity. Step 2 gave me some hope and the possibility of making different choices with my behavior and my life. As a Bahá'í, this "Power" is God, but of course it connects with Him to include Bahá'u'lláh, the Covenant, the Administrative Institutions, and the community, all of which are beyond my own individual self. The collective wisdom in my Al-Anon group, as well, was powerful beyond myself, as was the knowledge of counselors I turned to with the encouragement and support of others.

Step 3

Made a decision to turn our will and our lives over to the care of God as we understood Him.

Step 3 was a challenge for me as I worked to overcome my distrust of the Being that I felt had been punishing me. I had to work to let go of the control that had been my survival tool. Here I relied on Al-Anon strongly, going back again and again to my sponsors and my group for help. As I had small successes in letting go of my attempts to control people and outcomes, my faith and trust strengthened.

As I started trying to understand this Step 3, I studied the concept of "submitting" my will to God. Submission was defined for me as surrendering without resistance, and it implied strict obedience. I started out in Al-Anon believing that turning my will over to the Will of God was something like a multiple-round giant wrestling match. When I found a Bahá'í prayer that asked God to help me grow "as a tender herb in the meadows of Thy grace, that the gentle winds of Thy will may stir me up and bend me into conformity with Thy pleasure" (*Prayers and Meditations of Bahá'u'lláh*, pg. 240), I gained a different, more serene perspective of this concept!

I learned that the results of submission were all good, not bad, and that contentment with God's Will would result in serenity. Giving my will to God helped me to be the person I wanted to be. Trying to reflect the virtues and qualities God asked me to brought me closer to Him. This type of surrendering helped me to be sincere in my actions. When I struggled with a high level of anxiety, I now understood that this was a symptom of not relying on God to take care of my family and me. I could also now see that when I stayed angry about and did not accept aspects of the past, I was also not accepting God's Will.

A key part of this step was to recognize that the intent was not for me to submit to the will of my husband or another unhealthy person. Allowing them to manipulate my life guaranteed destruction and instability. Submission to God's Will allowed me to be lovingly detached from extreme emotional involvement with the suffering of another person.

Step 4

Made a searching and fearless moral inventory of ourselves.

Taking a searching moral inventory in Step 4 was an incredibly strong blending of the guidance in the Bahá'í Faith and in Al-Anon for me. Bahá'u'lláh says to "Bring thyself to account each day" and "True loss is for him whose days have been spent in utter ignorance of his self." (*Hidden Words of Bahá'u'lláh*, Arabic No. 31; *Tablets of Bahá'u'lláh*, "Words of Wisdom" pg. 156) I used specific books that Al-Anon provided to examine my attitudes and behavior. This action helped me to see that I was neglecting myself physically, mentally, emotionally, and spiritually. I had become highly controlling and critical of others. I had stopped going to the dentist. I did not eat or sleep well. I didn't exercise. I stopped my education. My praying was sporadic.

Also very important, however, was the emphasis on the positives. An inventory had to include the things that I was doing right and well, or where at least I was making some progress forward. This increased my self-respect and gave me a foundation on which to build more positive qualities and actions. The inventory helped me understand that I had to put my recovery as the highest priority in my life, because my ability to sustain functioning relationships with God, my family, and my community were all dependent on my being healthy and able to handle my responsibilities.

Step 5

Admitted to God, to ourselves, and to another human being the exact nature of our wrongs.

Step 5 almost chased me out of the Al-Anon Program. Bahá'u'lláh teaches that we should not confess our sins to other human beings and look to them for absolution of sins; this is God's territory. In my concern about this step, I sent Al-Anon literature to my National Spiritual Assembly and asked for its guidance (See Appendix 2 pg. 83). The Assembly very lovingly encouraged me to simply use this step as an opportunity to increase my self-knowledge by sharing my life with another person. It felt this step would provide me with an objective perspective of myself and the interactions with the alcoholic. I then felt free to stay in Al-Anon because I had a way to work this step. The Assembly also encouraged me to use the strength of the 12-Step program to cope with the challenges in my life.

By turning to God as part of Step 5, I started to believe and feel that He really could still love me, that maybe He had not given up on me when I had let go of Him. I also started to wonder if it was possible to feel His forgiveness and acceptance.

A key purpose in this step is getting beyond denial and taking mountains of accumulated problems, mistakes, and sins from inside ourselves and shrinking them into perspective by shining the light of love, insight, and forgiveness onto them. One of the things I was told in Al-Anon was that my secrets would keep me sick. Keeping problems bottled up inside of me caused me to obsess about them and blow them up bigger and bigger until they felt in total control of my mind. Step 5 helped me to feel free. I was able to share everything from my life that I had held in for so many years with trusted friends and counselors.

Step 6

Were entirely ready to have God remove all these defects of character.

On first looking at this step most people would think it would be easy...why would anyone want to hang onto defects of character? Well, sometimes defects are like a comfortable pair of shoes or slippers—we are used to how they feel and fit. A new pair takes time to become used to, and change is sometimes difficult to accept. For me it also took time and education to understand what parts of my behavior were healthy and what parts were destructive. I was afraid in some cases that if the bad were taken away, there would be nothing left.

I finally understood that part of God's role in this process was to help me substitute virtues and positive behavior in the places where He had helped me get rid of the negatives. I needed to focus on building my higher nature and reducing the size of my lower nature. I could then finally detach enough to decide God could work on me!

"In man there are two natures; his spiritual or higher nature and his material or lower nature. In one he approaches God, in the other he lives for the world alone."

('Abdu'l-Bahá, Paris Talks, p. 60)

Step 7

Humbly asked Him to remove our shortcomings.

Humility is hard for a person with "know-it-all" and "I need to be right" attitudes, and asking for help did not come easily to me. Since our positive qualities are gifts from God, however, Who better to ask for help? At times I struggled with having faith that God really could remove defects of character. Once I got to the point of believing He could, though, I wanted it to be instantaneous, with all my defects removed at the snap of my fingers. The answer was that it was going to be a lifetime process...this was just a beginning step. The basic work was mine to do with God's guidance, inspiration, and the example of other's lives such as 'Abdu'l-Bahá, the son of Bahá'u'lláh, founder of the Bahá'í Faith. It has been helpful for me to keep Marzieh Gail's words in mind that she wrote about her mother's interactions with 'Abdu'l-Bahá:

> *Two things 'Abdu'l-Bahá taught her she often quoted in Persian: One was that He said to her Sabr kun; mithl-i-Man básh—be patient, be as I am. The other was when someone expressed discouragement to Him, saying they could not possible acquire all the qualities and virtues that Bahá'ís are directed to possess, and the Master replied Kam Kam. Rúz bih rúz—little by little; day by day. (*The Bahá'í World, *Vol. XII, p. 704, reprinted in* Dynamic Force of Example, *pp. 50-51)*

I came to picture virtues laid out on a straight line and balancing on a foundation of God and prayer. If I moved too far to the left, I was moving away from the virtue and into negative behavior. If I moved too far to the right, I was misusing the virtue by overdoing it; for instance, being so patient and accepting that I did not take action when necessary. Part of the challenge for me was the old perfectionism pattern. The Bahá'í Writings identify so many virtues to work on that trying to make progress on all of them at once can be very overwhelming. I finally identified a few to concentrate on the most. This kept the process manageable for me.

Part of the interesting challenge in the process of developing virtues is that when we identify a defect or virtue to work on, tests and difficulties and the people in our lives suddenly seem designed to help directly with the development...staying grateful for God's assistance in these cases was tough!

In addition to working on my character, Steps 5, 6, and 7 prompted me to look after such basic things as going to the doctor, getting a full night's sleep, and saying my daily Obligatory prayer. If I did not remember to look after the basics, my hunger, pain, or fatigue would become overwhelming and interfere with my emotional and spiritual well-being.

Step 8

Made a list of all persons we had harmed, and became willing to make amends to them all.

This step did not ask me to fix anything, simply reflect over my life to determine if there were people in the past or currently in my life who had been hurt by any of my words, attitudes, or actions. Some of these people became obvious during the inventory done in Step 4. Whereas Step 4 focused on my personal self-inventory, however, Step 8 helped me with doing an inventory of my relationships with others.

There was no doubt for me that in the mess of my life I had harmed a number of people. My family was shut out, and my husband's family was pulled into the insanity; I ignored and manipulated Jerry; subjected my daughter to confusion, neglect, and verbal abuse; abandoned my friends; and disrupted the Bahá'í community. I also added myself to the list, because there was no question I had done great harm to myself mentally, emotionally, physically, and spiritually. This list of people became my starting point for actually attempting to repair the harm done, as would address in Step 9. I came back to this step more than once, because God in His mercy showed me the list of people that I harmed on a gradual basis—it would have been too overwhelming to be aware of them all at once.

The next part of Step 8 was working on the willingness to repair the damage. This required that I get beyond my own excuses, rationalizations, and denial mechanisms to actually admit and accept that I had done harm. It was important that I keep the focus on my part of the problem, regardless of any harm done by the other person, since their behavior was not my responsibility. I then needed to forgive myself for the actions I had done, and begin to think lovingly of the other person. I also had to pray for both myself and the other person to be able to work through the problem and let it go. Only when I felt that I could approach making amends in a positive frame of mind, and without expectations about the other person's response, could I go on to the next step of taking action.

Step 9

Made direct amends to such people wherever possible, except when to do so would injure them or others.

Most people when they reach this step start to realize that a very significant amend to make is a change in behavior. There was no point in my approaching someone with an apology for my behavior if my behavior had not changed. When I approached someone, I had to be honest and forthright in admitting what I had done wrong and how sorry I was about it. When I did this, generally the other person accepted my apology, and the relationship improved as a result.

In some cases, such as the relationship with my mother-in-law who did not understand what was going on, the damage was too great for things to be totally resolved, but at least there was improvement in our relationship. In other cases, there was no response. A few years after the incident where I had sought shelter with a Bahá'í family, I wrote to them and expressed my sorrow at the disruption I had caused in their household and let them know of the positive improvements I had made in my life since then, but I received no reply. It is important to stress that their reply or lack of reply did not change the fact that I needed to share my thoughts with them. Years after that, through the Assembly I had met with, I was able to re-establish contact and thank both them and the Assembly for their help.

There was a struggle in situations where I was unable to make direct amends to people who had died or were unreachable. This is particularly true where I mistreated childhood friends that I had lost contact with many years before. All I could do in those cases was pray, and hope I would have a chance to approach them in the next world after I died.

Although I did not experience this, for some of my group members had to decide it would cause more harm than good if they initiated contact with someone they had harmed. This might be the case where there was danger or something like past infidelity in a marriage where more disunity in a marriage would be the result. In these cases, they trusted in God to forgive and heal, and let go and let Him.

Intrinsic to the processes in Step 8 and Step 9 was a commitment for me to be active in attendance and service with the Bahá'í community and the Al-Anon program. I also committed to seek counseling as needed. For me, all were necessary to keep me from re-visiting hell and subjecting those around me and myself to the resulting pain. Guilt for things I had done was such a huge weight to carry around. These steps allowed me to work through forgiving myself, asking for God's forgiveness, and then taking action to improve the relationships I had harmed. It was necessary for me to take responsibility for my attitudes, actions, and behavior, without taking on responsibility for the actions of others.

I had to look at the best ways to approach people, detach from their behavior and focus on mine, and detach from their response or lack of response to my attempts to make amends. Assemblies may need to understand that while they can ask people to try to address the negative consequences of their behavior, the people may not be successful in re-establishing unity in relationships depending on the response they receive from others. Where trust has been broken, often repeatedly, it may take a long time to re-build trustworthiness and confidence. And, sometimes, it just doesn't succeed.

Step 10

Continued to take personal inventory and when we were wrong promptly admitted it.

Sometimes this step was easy for me and sometimes it was hard. It required self-awareness and a willingness to be vulnerable with others. My natural inclination was simply to justify or defend my actions and speech or withdraw and ignore the problem. However, I learned that the resulting personal discomfort and guilt were not what I wanted to live with or hang onto for very long. At times, I deliberately decided to wait a period of time, usually overnight, so that I became calm, centered, and able to focus on my own behavior and not on that of the other person. Letting the matter go on longer than a day or two, however, was usually very uncomfortable. I found that when I was able to use this step, it improved relationships, reduced resentments—both my own and other people's—and prevented guilt from piling up. Often other people were so surprised by a prompt admission of fault and an apology, that they were very willing to set the matter to rest.

I had to be sure that this Step did not put me in the position of confessing, as Bahá'ís are forbidden to do this. The Universal House of Justice sheds the following light on the subject:

Shoghi Effendi sets the prohibition into context. His secretary has written on his behalf that we...are forbidden to confess to any person, as do the Catholics to their priests, our sins and shortcomings, or to do so in public, as some religious sects do. However, if we spontaneously desire to acknowledge we have been wrong in something, or that we have some fault of character, and ask another person's forgiveness or pardon, we are quite free to do so. Kitáb-i-Aqdas, *Notes* #58

Step 11

Sought through prayer and meditation to improve our conscious contact with God as we understood Him, praying only for knowledge of His will for us and the power to carry that out.

Step 11 was made so much easier for me because of the Bahá'í Faith; I felt so much richer for having the prayers and meditations that the Writings contain. Pairing these together with Al-Anon's literature, I started my days on-track with time spent reading and meditating on the contents and how to apply them in my life. I did not use any particular method. I simply sat quietly in my house looking out the window, or whenever possible I sat quietly outdoors. Al-Anon reminded me though that "conscious contact with God" had to continue throughout my day, so I regularly turned to Him in conversation and need as challenges to my serenity happened. I used the Greatest Name (*'Yá Bahá'u'l-Abhá; Alláh-u-Abhá*) frequently, breathing in and filling myself with it before answering the phone or door, handling a problem or crisis, or speaking to someone.

Praying for knowledge of God's Will for me put me in the frame of mind and soul necessary to be aware of His guidance through events and people in my life. I learned that coincidences are really His quiet miracles in our lives. If I prayed for His Will, it reminded me that insistence on my will, my control, and my way, often landed me in trouble. There are times when God's Will is often a frustrating thing to figure out. I am sure that I am not alone in often wishing that direct, clear conversation was possible, but He also gave us the gifts of mind, heart, and souls to figure out answers! When I became stuck on trying to figure out what He wanted me to do to serve Him, I tried things like the Five Steps of Prayer (see Appendix 2 pg. 69), consulting with others, and praying that road blocks would appear when I was going the wrong way. Confirmations usually occurred for me when the pathway I chose was the right one.

Step 12

Having had a spiritual awakening as the result of these Steps, we tried to carry this message to alcoholics[AA]/others [Al-Anon], and to practice these principles in all our affairs.

There is no question that working through these steps helped to awaken and affirm my need for having God and the Bahá'í Faith in my life. The Al-Anon program itself was a regular spiritual home for me as well, as together with its members I prayed, loved, cried, and grew. I became a different person than when this journey started. I became much, much better than I ever dreamed I would be. I thank God regularly that He led me to help, and that the help made it possible for me to be a steadfast member of both the Bahá'í Faith and also of Al-Anon as long as I needed it.

Part of the joy of having gone through this process is that I became able to extend a helping hand and share my experience, strength, and hope with other people in pain. I spoke at Al-Anon meetings, sponsored new members, and served the group as an officer. Sometimes new attendees were able to listen and get help; sometimes they were not. For those that were not, I hoped the seed would be planted, and that someday when they were ready, they would know where to turn to for support.

If something is a spiritual principle, then it can be applied no matter where I find myself and no matter who I am with at that moment. The things that I learned in Al-Anon became part of my daily life. The Bahá'í Faith is as necessary to me as breathing is to my body, so I practice it as part of my daily life. Both include being of service, regularly, and with love I gave back and continue to give back what so many people gave me.

At times Step 12 was a challenge for me because the Bahá'í Faith is less well known than Christianity, so I did not feel as free as some Al-Anon members do to casually say in a meeting that they go to church or hold onto Jesus. If I said anything to anyone even before or after the meeting that was specific to the Faith, it prompted questions, and then I was struggling with the Al-Anon guidelines of not discussing religion and avoiding influencing the religious faith of others. At times this lack of understanding of my beliefs made using a sponsor or being a sponsor a little more difficult when spiritual subjects arose. What I had to remember was to try to be my whole, healthy self to the best of my ability, and trust others to love me for myself.

SOME LESSONS LEARNED

I have walked through a lot of my life behaving like a "know-it-all," so pain and recovery helped me to be more humble in admitting that I could be teachable and that I could ask for help. I have also learned that my teachers are often unexpected and can appear anytime and anywhere. I remember vividly one evening walking into a meeting in a terrible state, desperately hoping that there would be help for me there. I was very upset to discover that the speaker that evening was a Catholic nun, and I almost walked back out of the room. After all, what could a Catholic nun know about husband problems or my pain. I resignedly sat down, however, and then proceeded to hear one of the most inspiring, helpful stories of my life. This also taught me that I cannot assume someone cannot learn from me...God has put me in some unlikely circumstances that have had surprising outcomes.

I have observed that it is important to ensure that any group or therapist that a Bahá'í turns to in search of recovery is familiar with and supportive of the teachings of the Faith. Being involved with something that is contrary to the teachings can set up worse psychological problems and more estrangement for the Faith in the long run.

…[W]hile there is an appropriate role in the Bahá'í community for groups of individuals to come together to help each other to understand and to deal with certain problem situations, according to the Bahá'í Teachings there can be no place in our community for groups which actively promote a style of life that is contrary to the Teachings of the Cause."
(The Universal House of Justice to the National Spiritual Assembly of the Bahá'ís of the United States, September 11, 1995)

You should feel under no obligation to continue to consult with someone in whom you have lost confidence or who you believe may cause you to act contrary to the teaching of the Faith. However, it should be understood that counselling of the type you are receiving may cause a variety of emotions to surface as a normal part of the therapy. Individuals sometimes feel close attachment to their therapist or experience other feelings which might be unsettling because they are unexpected; such emotions may simply represent a beginning of helpful change and need prove no danger to one's moral standards.
(On behalf of the Universal House of Justice to an individual believer, September 7, 1990)

The journey of personal transformation is different for each individual. Getting help through marrying and living with someone very ill was in many ways a transformational gift. It reconnected me to Bahá'u'lláh, and it gave me a daughter I love very much. She has gone through her own journey and healing and is now happily married with children. My marriage survived many years through the difficulties; however, it did not ultimately stay intact. In spite of this, the lessons learned have contributed to my life immensely, and they continue to contribute through me to the lives of others.

BUILDING A SUPPORTIVE COMMUNITY

Often there are people who feel out-of-control inside themselves, feel they have not had control over bad things happening to them in the past, or do not feel they have enough control over their own lives in the present. As a result, they may show anxious, rigid, destructive, or compulsive behavior externally to others. This may manifest itself in destructive ways in the Bahá'í community as well. An individual might refuse to let others contribute food dishes to a community meal and do it all by him/herself so it's done the way it must be done. Someone might insist that every Spiritual Assembly meeting be at the same time, day, and place each week with everyone sitting in the same place every meeting. A person might not be able to spontaneously join in an activity, but instead only attend those that are carefully scheduled and planned. If an activity is not going according to the individual's expectations, her/his behavior might become angry, disruptive, or attacking. If meetings do not start exactly on time, a compulsive person might choose to stop coming at all. Someone else might be overly sensitive, crying easily or taking everything said in consultation very personally. Another person might lie to community members about things he/she said or did to exert unhealthy influence, hide actions, or give the illusion that they are in control.

These types of behaviors are often linked to very low self-respect, family-of-origin problems, and an inability to reach out in healthy ways to other people. These limitations often leave people feeling that they do not have choices to make things better. Fear of failure is a constant companion. Negative behavior and attitudes cause barriers that keep others away. Individuals and families become afraid of judgments and stigma, and declaration of belief in Bahá'u'lláh is not seen as an option. Alternatively, if belief is declared, distance from or withdrawal from the community is frequent and probable. Often individuals and families challenged by illnesses can be significantly helped by therapy or support groups, especially those called "12-Step Programs." Unfortunately, however, some Bahá'ís have adopted the attitude, and will frankly offer their opinion, that if people would only study the Bahá'í Faith or just pray more, that's all they would need; support groups or therapists are not really necessary.

There are a few problems with this position. First, this message tells suffering people that they are obviously spiritually inadequate, since they are finding the need to get help from something other than the Faith. It assumes that the person is healthy enough to be able to study the Writings and pray and get the needed help from this source. It ignores Bahá'u'lláh's guidance to seek help for healing. It assumes that there is no truth anywhere other than in the Bahá'í Writings. It ignores Shoghi Effendi's and the Universal House of Justice's guidance to alcoholics about turning to Alcoholics Anonymous (AA), which has been the foundation group for various 12-Step Programs (see Appendix 2, page 66).

Here are some quotations that provide insight into this matter:

> There are two ways of healing sickness, material means and spiritual means. The first is by the treatment of physicians; the second consisteth in prayers offered by the spiritual ones to God and in turning to Him. Both means should be used and practised. Illness which occur by reason of physical causes should be treated by doctors with medical remedies; those which are due to spiritual causes disappear through spiritual means. Thus an illness caused by affliction, fear, nervous impressions, will be helped more effectively by spiritual rather than by physical treatment. Hence, both kinds of treatment should be followed; they are not contradictory. Therefore thou shouldst also accept physical remedies inasmuch as these too have come from the mercy and favor of God, Who hath revealed and made manifest medical science so that His servants may profit from this kind of treatment also. Thou shouldst give equal attention to spiritual treatments, for they produce marvelous effects. Now, if thou wishest to know the true remedy which will heal man from all sickness and will give him the health of the divine kingdom, know that it is the precepts and teachings of God. Focus thine attention upon them.
>
> ('Abdu'l-Bahá, Lights of Divine Guidance, #923)

> As you know, Bahá'u'lláh has ordained that in case of illness we should always consult the most competent physicians. And this is exactly what the Guardian strongly advises you to do. For prayer alone is not sufficient. To render it more effective we have to make use of all the physical and material advantages which God has given us. Healing through purely spiritual forces is undoubtedly as inadequate as that which materialist physicians and thinkers vainly seek to obtain by

resorting entirely to mechanical devices and methods. The best result can be obtained by combining the two processes: spiritual and physical.

(*Shoghi Effendi, The Throne of the Inner Temple, p. 76*)

Experience seems to suggest that the healing process can often be a lengthy and stressful one requiring the close guidance and help of trained professionals. Advice given by well-meaning believers to the effect that you should seek to transcend psychological problems does not qualify as competent advice on what is essentially a medical issue.

(*On behalf of the Universal House of Justice to an individual believer, October 23, 1994*)

You are encouraged to follow the advice of your therapist in regard to the absences which you should take from your employment in order to facilitate your healing from the trauma you experienced in the past. The time taken away from work beneficial to society would doubtless be more than compensated for by the increase in effectiveness with which you will be able to perform such functions when your healing is more advanced.

(*On behalf of the Universal House of Justice to an individual believer, December 22, 1992*)

You have asked what to do since psychological problems sometimes make it difficult for you to participate in community events and Assembly meetings. In striving to follow the Teachings and the best medical advice you can obtain, you will want to remember that the healing you do now is an investment that will enable you to better serve in the future. Ideally, you would combine concentrating on healing with avenues of service which do not interfere with it.

(*On behalf of the Universal House of Justice to an individual believer, October 23, 1994*)

There is widespread uncertainty about whether alcoholism in particular is a disease or not. The American Medical Association refers to it in this manner, so I have done the same. The Institutions of our Faith remind us, however, that the laws of Bahá'u'lláh are clear that the standard is abstinence from alcohol and hallucinogenic drugs. This puts these issues into an area of morality in addition to one often requiring medical or counseling assistance. Local Spiritual Assemblies, must, therefore often guide and counsel individuals step-by-step towards obedience. Often this requires loving patience as the individuals experience relapses and struggle to obey. Greater knowledge and sensitivity will hopefully assist Assemblies in working with these individuals in such a way that their connections with the Assembly, community, and Bahá'u'lláh are maintained without them becoming estranged.

As a general rule, we are not in a position to determine whether someone is an "active" or an "inactive" Bahá'í. Nor can we make the diagnosis of someone's disease for them, although we can identify symptoms and help the individual and community to overcome any denial that there is a problem present. As I have illustrated, circumstances such as mine can affect the involvement of a community member. Getting help and support made it possible for me to be more connected. Understanding why someone is not attending community activities helps, and offering assistance where appropriate, is important.

One thing to understand is that there are many times when a person needs to be less active in Bahá'í or family activities for a period or periods of time in order to strongly focus on the recovery process. If this is not done, the person may not be able to be a healthy, contributing member of the community in the long run. Community and Assembly understanding and support of this process is important. As a wise friend of mine once said, "How can I possibly be effective in helping to build the institutions of world order if my life is unmanageable? How can I help the people in the world to overcome the institutional insanity of war and mis-allocation of resources if my own mind is out of order?"

Another important point for people to understand when interacting with individuals needing help or involved in recovery programs is that what is normally virtuous behavior is often not positive in addiction circumstances. What is kind, compassionate, and forgiving in most circumstances, can often be considered quite cruel in these cases. It is generally considered important that an addicted individual be held responsible and accountable for his/her actions. If the kindness of someone's heart prompts them to rescue the individual, cover up for actions caused by the addiction, or allow themselves to suffer the consequences instead, this often enables the suffering and addictive behavior to continue that much longer. In reality, this often extends their circumstance into being a much more serious problem.

A few examples of this phenomenon might help you with understanding what this means. If a community member is put in jail because they were drinking or using drugs and driving, the kindest thing is usually to leave them in, not bail them out, thereby helping them understand that there are serious consequences to their actions. If an Assembly Treasurer is not keeping the financial records in order because they are drinking, the most compassionate thing the Assembly might do is ask them to resign as an officer and get help, not let them keep on doing the job with the Assembly overlooking the problem. If two friends commit to attending an event, and one does not follow through because of an addiction problem, the first friend needs to follow through with the plans and go, not be deprived of the experience because of the disease.

This quotation might be helpful to shed some light on this principle as well:

> O ye beloved of the Lord! The Kingdom of God is founded upon equity and justice, and also upon mercy, compassion, and kindness to every living soul. Strive ye then with all your heart to treat compassionately all humankind—except for those who have some selfish, private motive, or some disease of the soul. Kindness cannot be shown the tyrant, the deceiver, or the thief, because, far from awakening them to the error of their ways, it maketh them to continue in their perversity as before. No matter how much kindliness ye may expend upon the liar, he will but lie the more, for he believeth you to be deceived, while ye understand him but too well, and only remain silent out of your extreme compassion.
>
> ('Abdu'l-Baha, Selections from the Writings of 'Abdu'l-Baha, #138)

Although many troubled or sick individuals are not involved in breaking Bahá'í laws, many are. There can be difficult spiritual consequences as a result.

> *Another example would involve, not a single offence, but a continuing course of behavior, such as flagrant and continuing violation of the law prohibiting the consumption of alcoholic beverages. In such a situation the Assembly should explain the law to the believer, urge him to obey it, encourage and assist him and warn him if necessary. If the response in favorable there would, again be no need to deprive him of his administrative rights, but, if the believer is obdurate or continues in his course of misbehavior, he should according to the circumstances of each case, be warned and warned again, with increasing severity and a time set for him to rectify his conduct. If this produces no amelioration, he would have to lose his administrative rights.*
>
> *(Bahá'í Reference Library, on behalf of the Universal House of Justice to the National Spiritual Assembly of the Bahá'ís of Australia, December 9, 1991)*

Alcoholism will hopefully be less common when we have the Golden Age of Bahá'u'lláh centuries in the future. Will we someday see the Writings and people's love for Bahá'u'lláh as enough to stop people from ever taking a drink, and therefore ever becoming active alcoholics? Certainly, but in these times of transition, support groups like AA offer very important help. The Universal House of Justice in fact addresses this issue:

> *The Bahá'í community should feel free to call upon such agencies as Alcoholics Anonymous for assistance and upon public agencies who work with the problem, but must realize*

that the greatest healing of this social and individual disease is God's Cause which in its fullness will eliminate the causes of alcoholism.....there is no objection to Bahá'ís being members of Alcoholics Anonymous, which is an association that does a great deal of good in assisting alcoholics to overcome their lamentable condition.

(On behalf of the Universal House of Justice, letter to an individual, November 5, 1987)

APPENDICES

APPENDIX 1: PRAYER FOR PURITY

O Divine Providence! Bestow Thou in all things purity and cleanliness upon the people of Bahá. Grant that they be freed from all defilement, and released from all addictions. Save them from committing any repugnant act, unbind them from the chains of every evil habit, that they may live pure and free, wholesome and cleanly, worthy to serve at Thy Sacred Threshold and fit to be related to their Lord. Deliver them from intoxicating drinks and tobacco, save them, rescue them, from this opium that bringeth on madness, suffer them to enjoy the sweet savors of holiness, that they may drink deep of the mystic cup of heavenly love and know the rapture of being drawn ever closer unto the Realm of the All-Glorious. For it is even as Thou has said: 'All that thou hast in thy cellar will not appease the thirst of my love—bring me, O cup-bearer, of the wine of the spirit a cup full as the sea!'

'Abdu'l-Bahá

Selections from the Writings of 'Abdu'l-Bahá, #129

APPENDIX 2:

GUIDANCE FROM BAHÁ'Í INSTITUTIONS AND THE BAHÁ'Í WORLD CENTRE RESEARCH DEPARTMENT

Item 1: Consultation for Problems; Confession

Your letter of 14 February 1973 enquiring about the uses of Bahá'í consultation has been received.

This is, of course, a matter in which rigidity should be avoided.

When a believer has a problem concerning which he must make a decision, he has several courses open to him. If it is a matter that affects the interests of the Faith he should consult with the appropriate Assembly or committee, but individuals have many problems which are purely personal and there is no obligation upon them to take such problems to the institutions of the Faith; indeed, when the needs of the teaching work are of such urgency it is better if the friends will not burden their Assemblies with personal problems that they can solve by themselves.

A Bahá'í who has a problem may wish to make his own decision upon it after prayer and after weighing all the aspects of it in his own mind; he may prefer to seek the counsel of individual friends or of professional counsellors such as his doctor or lawyer so that he can consider such advice when making his decision; or in a case where several people are involved, such as a family situation, he may want to gather together those who are affected so that they may arrive at a collective decision. There is also no objection whatever to a Bahá'í's asking a group of people to consult together on a problem facing him.

It should be borne in mind that all consultation is aimed at arriving at a solution to a problem and is quite different from the sort of group baring of the soul that is popular in some circles these days and which borders on the kind of confession that is forbidden in the Faith. On the subject of confession the Guardian's secretary wrote on his behalf to an individual believer: "We are forbidden to confess to any person, as do the Catholics to their priests, our sins and shortcomings, or to do so in public, as some religious sects do. However, if we spontaneously desire to acknowledge we have been wrong in something, or that we have some fault of character, and ask another person's forgiveness or pardon, we are quite free to do so. The Guardian wants to point out, however, that we are not obliged to do so. It rests entirely with the individual."

Universal House of Justice to the National Spiritual Assembly of Canada, March 19, 1973
Lights of Guidance, #589

Item 2: Directing the Course of One's Life

Each individual is unique and has a unique path to tread in his lifetime. In espousing the Bahá'í Faith you have defined the direction of that path, for your recognition of God's Manifestation for this Day and your devotion to His Message provide the spiritual and ethical basis for all aspects of your life of service to mankind, while the continuing guidance that He has provided for the community of His followers enables you to know the directions in which the most effort is required at the present time.

While, during the early years of the development of the Faith, Bahá'u'lláh, 'Abdu'l-Bahá and Shoghi Effendi sometimes gave specific instructions to individual believers on how they should serve the Cause, the Universal House of Justice seldom does this. It is, indeed, the precious privilege of the individual human being to direct the course of his own life. Through exercising this privilege while striving always to conform his conduct to the divine Teachings and devote his talents in the best possible way to the service of the Cause and mankind, a soul deepens his understanding of God and His will.

This does not mean that you are left to make your decisions without guidance. This you will find from several sources. Firstly, in general, you will find it in the Writings. Secondly, and more specifically, in the teaching plans issued by the Universal House of Justice. Thirdly, in the plans and projects of your own National Spiritual Assembly. All these, it would seem from your letter, you have been striving to follow. Fourthly, with regard to your own personal goals and actions, is the guidance you can receive through consultation—with your wife, with friends of your choice whose opinions you value, with your Local Spiritual Assembly, with such committees of your National Assembly as are concerned with the fields of activity towards which your inclinations lie. Fifthly, there is prayer and meditation.

You mention that the answers to your prayers never seem to have come through clearly. Mrs Ruth Moffett has published her recollection of five steps of prayer for guidance that she was told by the beloved Guardian. When asked about these notes, Shoghi Effendi replied, in letters written by his secretary on his behalf, that the notes should be regarded as "Personal suggestions," that he considered them to be "quite sound," but that the friends need not adopt them 'strictly and universally."

The House of Justice feels that they may be helpful to you and, indeed, you may already be familiar with them. They are as follows:

... use these five steps if we have a problem of any kind for which we desire a solution, or wish help.

Pray and meditate about it. Use the prayers of the Manifestations, as they have the greatest power. Learn to remain in the silence of contemplation for a few moments. During this deepest communion take the next step.

Arrive at a decision and hold to this. This decision is usually born in a flash at the close or during the contemplation. It may seem almost impossible of accomplishment, but if it seems to be an answer to prayer or a way of solving the problem, then immediately take the next step.

Have determination to carry the decision through. Many fail here. The decision, budding into determination, is blighted and instead becomes a wish or a vague longing. When determination is born, immediately take the next step.

Have faith and confidence, that the Power of the Holy Spirit will flow through you, the right way will appear, the door will open, the right message, the right principle or the right book will be given to you. Have confidence, and the right thing will come to meet your need. Then as you rise from prayer take immediately the fifth step.

Act as though it had all been answered. Then act with tireless, ceaseless energy. And, as you act, you yourself will become a magnet which will attract more power to your being, until you become an unobstructed channel for the Divine Power to flow through you.

Also the Guardian's secretary wrote to an individual believer on his behalf: "The Master said guidance was when the doors opened after we tried. We can pray, ask to do God's will only, try hard, and then if we find our plan is not working out, assume it is not the right one, at least for the moment."

On behalf of the Universal House of Justice,
Messages 1963 to 1986, p. 383

Item 3: Understanding Spiritual Guidance

God has endowed human beings with more than one way of receiving guidance in the decisions we have to make, as 'Abdu'l-Bahá has explained. There are the Holy Writings, in which are clear directions for the way in which we should live; if an inner voice prompts us to act contrary to the explicit teachings we can be sure that, far from being an inspiration from God, that inner voice is the expression of our own lower nature, and should be disregarded. There is also the gift of intelligence and good judgement—the faculty which distinguishes man from the animal kingdom; God intends us to use this faculty, which can be a powerful instrument for distinguishing between true inspirations and vain imaginings. There is the power of prayer through which we strive to purify our motives, to seek the Will of God and to implore His guidance and assistance. There is also the law of consultation, one of the distinguishing features of this great Revelation.

Consultation is to be used not only in the functioning of the Administrative Order, but is also available for the individual in solving his own problems; he may consult with his Assembly, with his family and with his friends.

Thus, in solving the problems which now confront you, the House of Justice urges you to worry less about the desirability of following what you perceive to be inspiration, and to bring to bear the other methods that God has given for the solution of difficulties. It suggests that you consult your Spiritual Assembly or an Auxiliary Board member or, if you have close friends whose judgement you respect, consult with them and pay careful attention to their advice....

On behalf of the Universal House of Justice
to an individual believer, November 29, 1982

Item 4:
Violence and the Sexual Abuse of Women and Children

Further to our letter of 14 November 1991, the Universal House of Justice has now completed its consideration of your letter of 21 September 1991, in which you raised a number of questions pertaining to violence and to the sexual abuse of women and children. We have been instructed to provide the following response to your questions.

As you know, the principle of the oneness of mankind is described in the Bahá'í Writings as the pivot round which all the Teachings of Bahá'u'lláh revolve. It has widespread implications which affect and remold all dimensions of human activity. It calls for a fundamental change in the manner in which people relate to each other, and the eradication of those age-old practices which deny the intrinsic human right of every individual to be treated with consideration and respect.

Within the family setting, the rights of all members must be respected. 'Abdu'l-Bahá has stated:

The integrity of the family bond must be constantly considered and the rights of the individual members must not be transgressed. The rights of the son, the father, the mother—none of them must be transgressed, none of them must be arbitrary. Just as the son has certain obligations to his father, the father, likewise, has certain obligations to his son. The mother, the sister and other members of the household have their certain prerogatives. All these rights and prerogatives must be conserved....

The use of force by the physically strong against the weak, as a means of imposing one's will and fulfilling one's desires, is a flagrant transgression of the Bahá'í Teachings. There can be no justification for anyone compelling another, through the use of force or through the threat of violence, to do that to which the other person is not inclined. 'Abdu'l-Bahá has written, "O ye lovers of God! In this, the cycle of Almighty God, violence and force, constraint and oppression, are one and all condemned." Let those who, driven by their passions or by their inability to exercise discipline in the control of their anger, might be tempted to inflict violence on another human being be mindful of the condemnation of such disgraceful behavior by the Revelation of Bahá'u'lláh.

Among the signs of moral downfall in the declining social order are the high incidence of violence within the family, the increase in degrading and cruel treatment of spouses and children, and the spread of sexual abuse. It is essential that the members of the community of the Greatest Name take utmost care not to be drawn into acceptance of such practices because of their prevalence. They must be ever mindful of their obligation to exemplify a new way of life distinguished by its respect for the dignity and rights of all people, by its exalted moral tone, and by its freedom from oppression and from all forms of abuse.

Consultation has been ordained by Bahá'u'lláh as the means by which agreement is to be reached and a collective course of action defined. It is applicable to the marriage partners and within the family, and indeed, in all areas where believers participate in mutual decision making. It requires all participants to express their opinions with absolute freedom and without apprehension that they will be censured or their views belittled; these prerequisites for success are unattainable if the fear of violence or abuse is present.

A number of your questions pertain to the treatment of women, and are best considered in light of the principle of the equality of the sexes which is set forth in the Bahá'í Teachings. This principle is far more than the enunciation of admirable ideals; it has profound implications in all aspects of human relations and must be an integral element of Bahá'í domestic and community life. The application of this principle gives rise to changes in habits and practices which have prevailed for many centuries. An example of this is found in the response provided on behalf of Shoghi Effendi to a question whether the traditional practice whereby the man proposes marriage to the woman is altered by the Bahá'í Teachings to permit the woman to issue a marriage proposal to the man; the response is, "The Guardian wishes to state that there is absolute equality between the two, and that no distinction or preference is permitted...." With the passage of time, during which Bahá'í men and women endeavor to apply more fully the principle of the equality of the sexes, will come a deeper understanding of the far-reaching ramifications of this vital principle. As 'Abdu'l-Bahá has stated, "Until the reality of equality between man and woman is fully established and attained, the highest social development of mankind is not possible."

The Universal House of Justice has in recent years urged that encouragement be given to Bahá'í women and girls to participate in greater measure in the social, spiritual and administrative activities of their communities, and has appealed to Bahá'í women to arise and demonstrate the importance of their role in all fields of service to the Faith.

For a man to use force to impose his will on a woman is a serious transgression of the Bahá'í Teachings. 'Abdu'l-Bahá has stated that:

The world in the past has been ruled by force, and man has dominated over woman by reason of his more forceful and aggressive qualities both of body and mind. But the balance is already shifting; force is losing its dominance, and mental alertness, intuition, and the spiritual qualities of love and service, in which woman is strong, are gaining ascendancy.

Bahá'í men have the opportunity to demonstrate to the world around them a new approach to the relationship between the sexes, where aggression and the use of force are eliminated and replaced by cooperation and consultation. The Universal House of Justice has pointed out in response to questions addressed to it that, in a marriage relationship, neither husband nor wife should ever unjustly dominate the other, and that there are times when the husband and the wife should defer to the wishes of the other, if agreement cannot be reached through consultation; each couple should determine exactly under what circumstances such deference is to take place.

From the Pen of Bahá'u'lláh Himself has come the following statement on the subject of the treatment of women:

> The friends of God must be adorned with the ornament of justice, equity, kindness and love. As they do not allow themselves to be the object of cruelty and transgression, in like manner they should not allow such tyranny to visit the handmaidens of God. He, verily, speaketh the truth and commandeth that which benefiteth His servants and handmaidens. He is the Protector of all in this world and the next.

No Bahá'í husband should ever beat his wife, or subject her to any form of cruel treatment; to do so would be an unacceptable abuse of the marriage relationship and contrary to the Teachings of Bahá'u'lláh.

The lack of spiritual values in society leads to a debasement of the attitudes which should govern the relationship between the sexes, with women being treated as no more than objects for sexual gratification and being denied the respect and courtesy to which all human beings are entitled. Bahá'u'lláh has warned: "They that follow their lusts and corrupt inclinations, have erred and dissipated their efforts. They, indeed, are of the lost." Believers might well ponder the exalted standard of conduct to which they are encouraged to aspire in the statement of Bahá'u'lláh concerning His "true follower," that: "And if he met the fairest and most comely of women, he would not feel his heart seduced by the least shadow of desire for her beauty. Such an one, indeed, is the creation of spotless chastity. Thus instructeth you the Pen of the Ancient of Days, as bidden by your Lord, the Almighty, the All-Bountiful."

One of the most heinous of sexual offenses is the crime of rape. When a believer is a victim, she is entitled to the loving aid and support of the members of her community, and she is free to initiate action against the perpetrator under the law of the land should she wish to do so. If she becomes pregnant as a consequence of this assault, no pressure should be brought upon her by the Bahá'í institutions to marry. As to whether she should continue or terminate the pregnancy, it is for her to decide on the course of action she should follow, taking into consideration medical and other relevant factors, and in the light of the Bahá'í Teachings. If she gives birth to a child as a result of the rape, it is left to her discretion whether to seek financial support for the maintenance of the child from the father; however, his claim to any parental rights would, under Bahá'í law, be called into question, in view of the circumstances.

The Guardian has clarified, in letters written on his behalf, that "The Bahá'í Faith recognizes the value of the sex impulse," and that "The proper use of the sex instinct is the natural right of every individual, and it is precisely for this very purpose that the institution of marriage has been established." In this aspect of the marital relationship, as in all others, mutual consideration and respect should apply. If a Bahá'í woman suffers abuse or is subjected to rape by her husband, she has the right to turn to the Spiritual Assembly for assistance and counsel, or to seek legal protection. Such abuse would gravely jeopardize the continuation of the marriage, and could well lead to a condition of irreconcilable antipathy.

You have raised several questions about the treatment of children. It is clear from the Bahá'í Writings that a vital component of the education of children is the exercise of discipline. Shoghi Effendi has stated, in a letter written on his behalf about the education of children, that:

Discipline of some sort, whether physical, moral or intellectual is indeed indispensable, and no training can be said to be complete and fruitful if it disregards this element. The child when born is far from being perfect. It is not only helpless, but actually is imperfect, and even is naturally inclined towards evil. He should be trained, his natural inclinations harmonized, adjusted and controlled, and if necessary suppressed or regulated, so as to ensure his healthy physical and moral development. Bahá'í parents cannot simply adopt an attitude of non-resistance towards their children, particularly those who are unruly and violent by nature. It is not even sufficient that they should pray on their behalf. Rather they should endeavor to inculcate, gently and patiently, into their youthful minds such principles of moral conduct and initiate them into the principles and teachings of the Cause with such tactful and loving care as would enable them to become "true sons of God" and develop into loyal and intelligent citizens of His Kingdom....

While the physical discipline of children is an acceptable part of their education and training, such actions are to be carried out "gently and patiently" and with "loving care," far removed from the anger and violence with which children are beaten and abused in some parts of the world. To treat children in such an abhorrent manner is a denial of their human rights, and a betrayal of the trust which the weak should have in the strong in a Bahá'í community.

It is difficult to imagine a more reprehensible perversion of human conduct than the sexual abuse of children, which finds its most debased form in incest. At a time in the fortunes of humanity when, in the words of the Guardian, "The perversion of human nature, the degradation of human conduct, the corruption and dissolution of human institutions, reveal themselves ... in their worst and most revolting aspects," and when "the voice of human conscience is stilled," when "the sense of decency and shame is obscured," the Bahá'í institutions must be uncompromising and vigilant in their commitment to the protection of the children entrusted to their care, and must not allow either threats or appeals to expediency to divert them from their duty. A parent who is aware that the marriage partner is subjecting a child to such sexual abuse should not remain silent, but must take all necessary measures, with the assistance of the Spiritual Assembly or civil authorities if necessary, to bring about an immediate cessation of such grossly immoral behavior, and to promote healing and therapy.

Bahá'u'lláh has placed great emphasis on the duties of parents toward their children, and He has urged children to have gratitude in their hearts for their parents, whose good pleasure they should strive to win as a means of pleasing God Himself. However, He has indicated that under certain circumstances, the parents could be deprived of the right of parenthood as a consequence of their actions. The Universal House of Justice has the right to legislate on this matter. It has decided for the present that all cases should be referred to it in which the conduct or character of a parent appears to render him unworthy of having such parental rights as that of giving consent to marriage. Such questions could arise, for example, when a parent has committed incest, or when the child was conceived as a consequence of rape, and also when a parent consciously fails to protect the child from flagrant sexual abuse.

As humanity passes through the age of transition in its evolution to a world civilization which will be illuminated by spiritual values and will be distinguished by its justice and its unity, the role of the Bahá'í community is clear: it must accomplish a spiritual transformation of its members, and must offer to the world a model of the society destined to come into being through the power of the Revelation of Bahá'u'lláh. Membership in the Bahá'í community is open to all who accept Bahá'u'lláh as the Manifestation of God, and who thereupon embark on the process of changing their conduct and refining their character. It is inevitable that this community will, at times, be subject to delinquent behavior of members whose actions do not conform to the standards of the Teachings. At such times, the institutions of the Faith will not hesitate to apply Bahá'í law with justice and fairness in full confidence that this Divine Law is the means for the true happiness of all concerned.

However, it should be recognized that the ultimate solution to the problems of humanity lies not in penalties and punishments, but rather in spiritual education and illumination. 'Abdu'l-Bahá has written:

It is incumbent upon human society to expend all its forces on the education of the people, and to copiously water men's hearts with the sacred streams that pour down from the Realm of the All-Merciful, and to teach them the manners of Heaven and spiritual ways of life, until every member of the community of man will be schooled, refined, and exalted to such a degree of perfection that the very committing of a shameful act will seem in itself the direst infliction and most agonizing of punishments, and man will fly in terror and seek refuge in his God from the very idea of crime, as something far harsher and more grievous than the punishment assigned to it.

It is toward this goal that the community of the Greatest Name is striving, aided and reinforced by the limitless power of the Holy Spirit.

On behalf of the Universal House of Justice to an individual, January 24, 1993

Item 5: Consultation and 12-Step Programs

The view has been put forth that the open expression of feelings and the honest expression of ideas are fundamental to productive Bahá'í consultation, and further, that the Alcoholics Anonymous (AA) 12-Step program can make an important contribution to honest and open communication. In this regard, guidance was sought concerning the expression of feelings in the course of consultation.

While there may well be similarities between elements of the process of consultation and the 12-Step program, they differ in their overall goals. The intent of the open expression by the individual as practiced in AA is, by and large, to effect a healing and a release from the habit of drinking. Consultation, on the other hand, has as its object "the investigation of truth".

The distinction between the purpose of consultation and therapeutic endeavors is made explicit in the following extracts from letters written by or on behalf of the Universal House of Justice:

It should be borne in mind that all consultation is aimed at arriving at a solution to a problem and is quite different from the sort of group baring of the soul that is popular in some circles these days and which borders on the kind of confession that is forbidden in the Faith.

From a letter dated 19 March 1973 from the Universal House of justice to a National Spiritual Assembly

In regard to your question about the fifth step in the "AA 12-Step Program", we have been asked to share with you the following extract from a letter written on behalf of the Universal House of Justice on 26 August 1986 to an individual believer:

...there is no objection to Bahá'ís being members of Alcoholics Anonymous, which is an association that does a great deal of good in assisting alcoholics to overcome their lamentable condition. The sharing of experience which the members undertake does not conflict with the Bahá'í prohibition of the confession of sins; it is more in the nature of the therapeutic relationship between a patient and a psychiatrist.

On behalf of the Universal House of Justice, letter to an individual, November 5, 1987; Issues Concerning Community Functioning, A Memorandum prepared by the Research Department of the Universal House of Justice

Item 6: Seeking Help from Al-Anon

The National Spiritual Assembly is grateful to you for your letter of 2 December 1981 and the pamphlets on Al-Anon. It has requested that we reply to you on its behalf.

The National Spiritual Assembly has over the years frequently suggested to those who have developed alcoholism to seek assistance from Alcoholics Anonymous as this organization has a fine record of successfully treating this disease. Many of its ideals and methods are in harmony with the Bahá'í Teachings and alcoholics can be strengthened spiritually as well as guided to the solution of their drinking problems.

It is quite understandable that the matter of confession would raise some doubts in your mind as Bahá'u'lláh's injunction against confession is very clear. However, this step in Al-Anon is not confession with the idea of being absolved of one's sins, but is rather a step which helps in self-knowledge. Bahá'u'lláh has said "True loss is for him whose days have been spent in utter ignorance of his self." (*Tablets of Bahá'u'lláh*, p. 156). Al-Anon as well as AA is a type of therapy, a therapy not based on medical practices but which stems from the need of human beings to solve their problems using basically spiritual concepts. We cannot expect a therapeutic method to work if the problems it is designed to address are not spelled out.

The inventory that is suggested as necessary would contain material relevant to the problems the alcoholic creates and the problems that those close to him create for him. This is not confession of sins as much as being as objective about your own personality and character. Sharing your evaluation of yourself with a close friend would not necessarily be a confession of wrong-doing to that friend as it would be asking someone who is more objective to help you come to a fuller understanding of yourself and your interactions with the alcoholic in your environment.

Taking steps which have proved effective in solving a serious problem is very commendable and we trust that through your sincere efforts and prayers yours and your husband's problems will be successfully resolved.

National Spiritual Assembly of the Bahá'ís of the United States, Office of the Secretary, to an individual believer, December 17, 1981

APPENDIX 3:

WARNING SIGNS OF AN ABUSER

It can be common for people to not recognize that they are interacting with an abuser until after they are deeply involved. The items below can be indicators to observe early on. Abuse can be mental, emotional, spiritual, or physical. The abuser is often male, but not always. Watch out and seek help when someone acts in these ways, especially when multiple indicators are present:

1. Shows unhealthy perfectionism with unreasonable and inflexible high standards, and a strong negative reaction when they feel disappointed in another person's actions
2. Criticizes and puts-down self and others
3. Displays emotional instability with extreme reactions
4. Manipulates with guilt, scorn, and shame
5. Refuses to accept responsibility for their actions or life
6. Behaves in an overly jealous way and attempts to restrict contact with other people
7. Focuses only on themselves and are unable to compassionately see others' perspectives
8. Contacts someone constantly and through multiple ways
9. Disrespects boundaries or personal space; engages in stalking behavior

10. Threatens to hurt themselves or others if some specific action is or is not taken
11. Insists on co-mingling and managing money on behalf of someone else
12. Appears to be putting on an act or behaves initially according to all the "proper relationships rules" but can't sustain it
13. Exerts strong pressure to move a relationship forward too fast
14. Behaves with cruelty towards animals and children
15. Displays rigidity about gender roles
16. "Accidentally" hurts others during intimate moments

APPENDIX 4:

ADDITIONAL 12-STEP RESOURCES

In the decades since Alcoholics Anonymous began, people have seen a wide variety of applications for the 12-Steps. These applications are both for the person directly challenged with a problem and for the family members and friends in their lives. There are now groups that address such addictions as food, sex, gambling, drugs, and so on. For a comprehensive list, please visit: https://en.wikipedia.org/wiki/List_of_twelve-step_groups

56715959R00054

Made in the USA
Middletown, DE
15 December 2017